The Big Fat Lies Recipes: 80 Delicious and Healthy Meals, Lose Weight Eating The Foods You Love

by John McDonalds

D1444532

Table of Contents

Bacon and Cheese Puffs

McDonalds Quiche

Bacon Cheeseburger Quiche

Bacon and Leek Quiche

HOT BACON DRESSING

Bacon and Egg Quiche

Bacon in Spinach Salad

Bacon in Toscana Soup

CHEESE AND BUTTER

Almond Butter Sponge cake

Buttery Cheesecake Bites

Crustless Breakfast Quiche

Pepperoni Frittata

Cheese Puffs

Cheese With Baked Cod

Stuffed Mozzarella

Delicious Cheese cube

Cottage Cheese Pie

Crab-Cheese Dip

Bacon Cheesecake Bites

McDonalds Chicken Cheese Dip

John's Cheese Ball

Quiche with Swiss cheese

Seductive Seafood Quiche

Creamy Cheesecake

Sprouts weds Cheddar

Orange Cheesecake

Cheese N Yoghurt

D' Best Cheesed Asparagus

Strawberry Cheesecake

Sumptuous Rarebit

Cheesy Spinach Casserole

EGGs AND MILK

McDonalds Devilled Eggs

Eggs Frittata

Southern Scotch Eggs

Southwestern Swiss Eggs

Cloud 9 Omelet

Sea Breeze Scrambled Eggs

Egg Drop Soup

Eggs Florentine

Egg with Mushroom Soufflés

Egg Custard

Ecstatic Egg Salad

Tasty Broccoli with Eggs

Italian Pie

Ultimate Egg Omelet

Spinach Cheese Pie

Tasty Chicken Egg Foo Young

POULTRY AND MEAT

Smoked Chicken Wrapped in Bacon

Melodious Meatloaf

McDonalds Skillet Meatloaf

The Ultimate Golumpki Casserole

Delicious Beef Tenderloin with cheese

Pepperoni Pizza

Sausage with Cabbage

Baked Zucchini Beef

Onion Supreme Burger

Simple Moussaka

The True Reason Why We Get Fat

Is fat around your tummy freaking you out? Are you tired of wasting money on stupid weight loss programs and drugs? Learn about the true reasons why we get fat...

Obesity is probably one of the most talked about and researched topics of the world. According to recent research studies, more than two-third people of America are overweight. In fact, the rate of obesity is skyrocketing in a faster rate and has become widespread. Scientists agree that obesity is becoming one of the most dangerous health problems. Not only do adults suffer from obesity, but teenagers and kids are also a target of this uncontrollable and panicking disease. Various ways have been devised to get rid of body fat, such as diet plans, diet pill, workouts, and weight loss drinks. You might have watched several catchy advertisements of weight loss products on television that claim to help you become slim in a few days or a week. Many of these products are either fraud or harmful. So it's important to tell yourself that instead of using these silly products, you should first focus on figuring out the true causes of becoming fat.

What Makes You Fat?

There would be scarcely a person on the earth who does not want to look beautiful, and when it comes to aesthetics, nothing can be more important than body weight. Many of you want to have attractive body figures like Hollywood stars, and for this reason, weight loss products have become very famous and expensive these days. However, using anti-obesity pills and drinks is not a wise idea. The best thing you can do to achieve your weight loss goals is understand the real causes of weight gain. Here are some major reasons that can cause weight gain in the body:

1. Genes

Most people suffer from obesity because of genetic reasons. Basically, your genes determine the way your body functions. In fact, you're different from other people due to your genes. It's true that you cannot change your genes. Though there are not clear evidences to prove that obesity is genetic, research studies and surveys show that it runs in families often times. Scientists are still working on these lines so as to discover the connection between obesity and genes.

2. Eating Habits

It goes without saying that your eating habits seriously affect your weight. Most people get fat because they eat wrong foods in wrong ways. It's important to eat healthy foods so as to maintain healthy weight of the body. While there are foods that help lose weight, there are others that cause speedy weight gain. Science proves that there are certain eating patterns that badly affect your figure. Some most common diet mistakes are:

- Fasting for several hours followed by eating a lot.
- Eating with a very fast speed.
- Emotional eating.
- Habitual eating.
- Pleasure eating.

3. An Inactive Lifestyle

Most people in America are fat because they are physically inactive. The major reason behind lack of physical activities is that people sit too much in front of televisions or computers. Unlike past, people don't spend leisure in sports and other outdoor activities. People use cars for traveling instead of walking. In fact, modern technologies have turned every other individual into a couch potato, and that's why obesity is becoming the world's most terrible health issue.

4. Environment

Your environment is also responsible for your eating habits. Sometimes, you get fat because you cannot access healthy food in your surroundings. Another reason could be unavailability of parks, gardens, and affordable gyms in your area. Restaurants and cafes in your locality also contribute to weight gain if they serve oversized food portions. Most Americans get fat because they watch catchy ads about food items and drinks on tv that trigger fast food lures in them.

5. Emotional Factors

Surprising but true! Your emotions are also involved in making you a fat individual. Most people eat food when they are free and have nothing else to do. It has also been seen that some people eat a lot when they are depressed or angry. Smoking, drinking, and pregnancy can also contribute to an increase in weight.

Other factors that can cause obesity include lack of sleep, use of medications, and medical conditions. So the next time you watch a crafty ad on TV, consult a medical professional before trying another weight loss product so as to figure out the true reason behind your weight gain.

Bad Calories, Good Calories: Discover the connection between fat consumption and obesity

Sick of your chubby face and fleshy buttocks? Tired of trying again and again? Weight loss efforts can surely drive anyone crazy. Sometimes, you do everything and stubborn fats do not go away. It's something that happens to almost everyone who is trying to get rid of extra weight. If you're on your way to develop slim figure, you should learn what calories to eat. Confused? Yes, it's true that all calories are not bad. Most people fail to maintain the desired weight because they stick to counting calories instead of knowing good and bad calories.

Developing deep understanding of what foods have good calories is crucial. It plays a great role in helping you choose the best foods throughout the week. Once you start making healthy food choices based on good calories, you will end up losing weight gradually. Including good calorie foods to your daily diet also helps improve overall health of the body. Good calorie foods satisfy your body's nutrient needs and that's why your emotional as well as physical health improves.

Avoid Empty Calories & Stay Healthy

In order to maintain healthy weight, you need to consume more calories than you take. This is only possible if you steer clear of empty calories. According to research studies, empty calories are responsible for adding a huge number of useless calories to the body. Empty calories do not provide body with the required nutrients. Those foods that is high in sugar and added fat fall into the category of empty calories. Sugary foods, bakery items, ice cream, and soft drinks are examples of empty calorie foods. In order to supply vitamins and minerals to the body, you should make sure to include whole foods to your diet. In other words, say NO to processed food items.

You might have grown up with the belief that FATS are always BAD. But here is a good news! You can enjoy fats even in healthy meals.

Why Fats Make You Fat?

Before learning what fats to include in your diet, you should first understand why eating fatty foods increases your weight. It's because of the fact that one gram of fat has almost twice as many calories as proteins and carbohydrates. Whether you want to maintain healthy weight or you're trying to get rid of extra pounds, you need to restrict your fat intake.

All Fats are Not Bad

If you have been on a weight loss program or diet, you might have come across this advice several times that you should avoid fatty foods. Yes, fatty foods can serve as stones in your path to a slim and smart figure. However, it's important for you to understand that all fats are not bad. While there are fats that affect your health negatively, there are others that improve it.

Those fatty foods that have trans and saturated fats in them are bad for your health.

The foods that contain processed and animal fats in them are considered as bad fat foods. Certain baked items, poultry skin, fried foods, red meat, and butter are a few examples of those foods that contain bad fats. Instead of eating these foods, try to include those foods in your diet that have unsaturated fats in them. Vegetable oils, like olive oils are the best sources of unsaturated fats. Fatty fish, such as salmon, mackerel, and tuna are also good for providing your body with omega-3 fatty acids. Likewise, nuts are also good for supplying good fats to the body.

Which Fats to Eat?

All fats do not make you fat. You need to discriminate between good and bad fats. Good fats are those fats that improve your health, such as unsaturated fats. On the other hand, fats, such as trans-fat and saturated fat are bad for your health because they have fewer minerals and vitamins in them. So you should try to keep track of which fats you eat. While trying to lose weight, you should not forget that you still have to count calories even when you eat good fats. It's because of the fact that extra calories lead to weight gain even if you get them from fat-free foods. This is because the body tends to store extra calories, which in turn leads to increase in weight.

So while you're struggling to lose weight, make sure that you're not just replacing high fat foods with high calorie foods. Otherwise, you're just wasting your time!

Fat; The Surprising truth about meat, cheese, whole milk, and eggs

Who does not love to melt a slice of butter over sirloin steaks? Most people are crazy about smothering butter on a freshly served hot plate of their favorite meal. And what about red meat? Be it pork belly or lamb chops, everyone enjoys eating it. It's a common myth among folks that eating fatty foods will make you fat. However, the latest research studies have proven it wrong. In fact, the foods you had been considering as weight increasing factories are actually gold mines of nutrients. So why not reverse the gear and turn back to dairy products? Of course, processed dairy items are not our topic of discussion.

The big fat surprise! Know why and how meat, cheese, whole milk, and eggs belong in a healthy meal...

Previously, people on weight loss programs used to exclude eggs, meat, butter, and cheese from their daily diet. This is not even uncommon these days. The slimmer still tend to unlike dairy products and want to keep them at bay. People avoid dairy products because of their high fat content.

However, recent research studies have shown that despite being rich in fat dairy products help trigger weight loss. These foods are especially effective when you're trying to lose weight from your midriff.

Is excluding dairy products from your diet a wrong way to get rid of extra weight? Strange facts about the connection between weight loss and dairy products revealed!

What's the Truth about Weight Loss and Dairy Products?

The latest scientific research studies have blown all myths about dairy products out of water. Today, dieticians believe that it's crucial for you to add eggs, cheese, yogurt, whole milk, and red meat to your daily diet. These foods have all those essential nutrients that your body needs in order to function properly. Dairy products are rich in vitamin B, Zinc, and protein. Moreover, they are packed with calcium, which is an essential mineral for building healthy and strong bones. Calcium deficiency in the body can cause bone thinning or osteoporosis.

According to some research studies almost 1 out of 2 women suffer from osteoporosis every year. Obviously, whole milk, meat, and eggs can make a great contribution to fat and calorie intake in the body. However, eating wisely and keeping calories in mind is the key to maintain healthy weight. You can also try low-fat dairy products, such as skimmed milk if you're too conscious about your fat intake. Low fat dairy products are good because they have more calcium as compare to full fat products.

Scientific research studies say that dairy products aid weight loss. Dairy products make a perfect calorie control diet for effective weight loss.

What Makes Meat, Cheese, Whole Milk, and Eggs Good for Weight Loss and Health?

Turning your bland meals into masterpieces is easy with dairy products. Formerly, dairy products had been blamed for almost every disease from heart attack to obesity. However, recent studies have reintroduced dairy products as healthy foods.

- ### Packed with Fat Soluble Vitamins

Dairy foods, such as milk, butter, and cheese are rich in fat soluble vitamins. Most dairy products contain vitamin E, K2, and A. When it comes to vitamin A and E, you can get them from a diet that includes plants and animals. However, most people are unaware that modern diet rarely contains vitamin K2 which can improve your health magically. K2 is related to calcium metabolism and its deficiency can lead to bone thinning, which in turn causes obesity.

- ### Linoleic Acid

Dairy products, such as butter are packed with conjugated linoleic acid, which is used in various weight loss supplements because of its miraculous effects on metabolism. Several research studies have shown that linoleic acid has been found to be effective in lowering fat content in the body.

- ### Rich in Saturated Fats

Dairy products are rich in saturated fats which are very good for the body. In the past, science used to consider saturated fats bad. However, the latest research studies have proven that saturated fats are perfectly harmless. It's been proved that saturated fats do not contribute to obesity and heart diseases.

LETs Get Started

These 80 Delicious, Mouthwatering and healthy foods, we have prepared; all which are Low in carbs, Low in Sugar, and in line with the Big fat surprise diet plan will help you get started in no time. Boost your metabolism, lose weight and enjoy a long healthy and happy life. You are free to tweak or substitute this recipes based on your personal preference.

We have tried our best to bring you the best Recipe for the Big fat Surprise diet plan, but sometimes, it's impossible to get it all right, So if you come across any error whatsoever in this book, please don't hesitate to send me a mail at johnMcDonalds@bigfatrecipes.com. Your thoughts and feedback is important to me and it's very much welcome.

Now on to the Recipes:

BACON

The middle cut of pork, upon being cured by smoking, is regarded as bacon. It is sometimes used for larding purposes, but as it contains leaner than salt pork, has a very pleasing flavor, and is the most easily digested fat known, it is much used for food. The strip of fat that occurs between the rind, or outer coat, and the first layer of lean is the firmest and the best for larding. The fat that fries out of bacon is excellent for use in the cooking and seasoning of other foods, such as vegetables and meats. When bacon is cooked for the table, its flavor will be improved if it is broiled rather than fried in its own fat. The rind of bacon should, as a rule, be trimmed off, but it should never be wasted, for it may be used to grease a pancake griddle or any pan in which food is to be cooked, provided the bacon flavor will not be objectionable.

In purchasing bacon, it is usually more economical to buy the whole side, or the entire middle cut, but if smaller quantities are desired, any amount, either in one piece or in slices, may be bought. The commercially cut bacon, which is very thin and becomes very crisp in its preparation, may be bought with the rind retained or removed. In both of these forms, it is often put up in jars or packed neatly in flat pasteboard boxes. While such bacon is undoubtedly the most popular kind, it should be remembered that the more preparation that is put on such a food before it enters the home, the more expensive it becomes. Very satisfactory results can be obtained from bacon bought in the piece if care is used in cutting it. To secure very thin, even slices, a knife having a thin blade that is kept sharp and in good condition should always be used.

BACON AND EGGS.--There are many combinations in which bacon is one of the foods, but no more palatable one can be found than bacon and eggs. This is generally a breakfast dish; still there is no reason why it cannot be used at times for luncheon or supper to give variety.

To prepare this combination of foods, first pan-broil the desired number of slices of bacon in a hot frying pan until they are crisp and then remove them to a warm platter. Into the fat that has fried out of the bacon, put the required number of eggs, which have first been broken into a saucer. Fry them until they reach the desired degree of hardness, and then remove to the platter containing the bacon. Serve by placing a slice or two of bacon on the plate with each egg.

Bacon N Cheddar Whipped Potatoes

Serves 4

Ingredients:

1 1/4 cup Cheddar, mild, grated
Salt and pepper to taste
4 strips Bacon, cooked, drained, and diced
4 large Potatoes, peeled and cut
1/2 cup (or more) Milk
2 Tablespoons Butter

How you make it:

1. Cook the potatoes in water until soft. Drain.
2. Then you place in a mixer bowl.
3. While the potatoes are still hot, add the butter and cheese.
4. Add a little milk and start the mixer on low.
5. Increase the speed and add milk as needed until the potatoes are fluffy and light.
6. Add the bacon and blend in well. Check seasonings. Serve warm.

Note: You can serve this hearty side dish with your favorite beef or pork entree.

Bacon Dog Roll-Ups

Serves 8

Ingredients:

1 lb. bacon cut in the middle
Brown sugar
16 hot dogs cut in half

How you make it:

1. Wrap a piece of bacon around each piece of hot dog.
2. Secure with a toothpick.
3. Place one layer in bottom of crock-pot and cover with sprinkles of brown sugar.
4. Repeat layering. Cook on low temperature for about 3 to 4 hours.

Bacon Blue Cheese Burgers

Serves 4
Ingredients:

4 leave green lettuce
1 tomato
1 1/4 lb. lean ground beef
1 Tbs. Onion flakes
4 Kaiser rolls
1/4 cup blue cheese, crumbled
1/4 cup cooked crumbled bacon
1 tsp. Montreal Steak Seasoning (or seasoning of choice)

How you make it:

1. Preheat George Foreman grill (you can use any available grill).
2. Wash and slice tomato into 1/8 inch slices.
3. Wash the lettuce leaves and separate into 4; then you set aside.
4. Slice Kaiser Rolls in half; set aside.
5. Place in mixing bowl; bacon, ground beef, steak seasoning, blue cheese and onions.
6. Gently fold ingredients together. Form into 4 equal patties.
7. Place patties on grill; close lid and grill for about 5-6 minutes. Assemble burgers with favorite toppings.

Bacon-Fried

Serves 4

Ingredients:

1 tsp. salt
1/2 cup flour
1/4 tsp. pepper
1/4 lb. bacon, cut into small pieces
2-1/2 to 3 lbs. chicken pieces

How you make it:

1. Mix flour, pepper and salt.
2. In flour mixture, coat the chicken.
3. In a ten inch skillet, Fry bacon partially.
4. Cook bacon and chicken over medium heat, until chicken is brown, for about 15-20 minutes, then you lower the heat.
5. Simmer while covered properly turning chicken once or twice, until thickest pieces are done, for about 20-30 minutes.
6. If skillet cannot be covered tightly, add 1-2 tablespoons water. Uncover and cook 10 minutes.

Bacon and Double Cheese Quiche

Serves 6

Ingredients:

4 large Eggs
10 strips Bacon
1/2 cup Water
1 cup Heavy Cream
1/8 teaspoon White Pepper
1/4 teaspoon dried Thyme
1/2 cup shredded White Cheddar cheese
1/2 cup shredded Gruyere cheese

How you make it:

1. Preheat oven to 375°F.
2. Cook bacon over medium heat until crisp or for approximately 8-10 minutes, in medium skillet.
3. Transfer to paper towel to drain.
4. Then Whisk together the eggs, cream, water, thyme and pepper, in a small bowl.
5. Pour into greased pie dish. Crumble bacon.
6. Sprinkle the egg mixture with the Gruyere cheese, bacon, and Cheddar. Back until golden and custard is set, for exactly 30 minutes. Allow to cook 10 minutes before slicing. Enjoy!

Tantalizing Crust-less Broccoli Quiche

Makes 8

Ingredients:

1 C. half & half
4 slices bacon
1 C. grated Swiss cheese
1/4 t. salt
1 C. Broccoli florets
A little white pepper
1/8 t, garlic powder
1/8 t. lemon pepper

How you make it:

1. Preheat to 350. Crisp bacon in microwave.
2. Beat eggs, add cheese and stir in broccoli, garlic powder salt and lemon pepper, in a bowl.
3. Stir in 1/2 of the bacon, pour into pie plate, un-greased and bake for about 30/35 minutes.
4. Top with remaining bacon. Serve cold, hot or at room temperature.
5. This meal is so tantalizing you can take it to work for lunch or a snack.

Note: Of course you may add and omit different cheeses, spinach in lieu of bacon

Bacon-Stuffed Eggs

Serves 8

Ingredients:

4 slices bacon, cooked and crumbled
12 large eggs
1 (3-ounce) package cream cheese, softened
2 teaspoons prepared horseradish
1/4 cup mayonnaise
2 teaspoons Worcestershire sauce
Garnish: chopped chives, if desired
1/2 teaspoon pepper

How you make it:

1. Place eggs in a large saucepan; add water to depth of 3 inches.
2. Bring to a boil; cover, remove from heat, and let stand 15 minutes. Drain immediately and fill the saucepan with cold water and ice.
3. Tap each egg firmly on the counter until cracks form all over the shell.
4. Peel under cold running water.
5. Slice eggs in half lengthwise and carefully remove yolks.
6. Mash yolks with mayonnaise. Add bacon and next 5 ingredients; stir well.
7. Spoon yolk mixture into egg whites. Garnish, if desired.

Bacon and Tomato Potato Skins

Serves 6

Ingredients:

2 tsp. cooking oil
6 large baking potatoes
1 tsp. chili powder
1/2 cup dairy sour cream (optional)
2/3 cup chopped Canadian-style bacon or chopped, cooked turkey bacon
Several dashes bottled hot pepper sauce
2 tbsp. finely chopped green onion
4 oz. cheddar cheese or reduced-fat cheddar cheese, shredded (1 cup)
1 medium tomato, finely chopped

How you make it:

1. Scrub potatoes thoroughly and prick with a fork.

2. Arrange on a microwave-safe plate. Micro-cook, uncovered, on 100% power (high) for 17 to 22 minutes or till almost tender, rearranging once. (Or, bake potatoes in a 425 degrees F. oven for 40 to 45 minutes or till tender.) Cool.

3. Share each potato into half lengthwise. Scoop out the inside of each potato half, leaving about a 1/4-inch-thick shell.

4. Cover and chill the leftover fluffy white part of potatoes for another use.

5. Combine the chili powder, cooking oil, and hot pepper sauce.

6. With a pastry brush, brush the insides of the potato halves with the oil mixture.

7. Cut the potato halves in half lengthwise. Return to the baking sheet.

8. Sprinkle potato quarters with bacon, tomato, and green onion.

9. Top with cheese. To make ahead, cover and chill for a day up to 24 hours.

10. Bake in 450 degrees F. oven until cheese is melted, or for 10 to 12 minutes and potato quarters are heated through.

11. Serve with sour cream, if desired.

Bacon n Beef Burgundy

Serve 3

Ingredients:

6 small pearl onions cut into fourths
1/4 lb. mushrooms, sliced
3 Tbsp. butter
1 lb. Top Sirloin steak, cut into 1" cubes or 1 pkg. Tenderloin tips, cut in cubes
1/4 lb. bacon, diced
1 tbsp. flour
3/4 cup beef broth
1/2 cup Burgundy wine
1 bay leaf
1/2 tsp. ground thyme
1 1/2 cups carrots, diagonally sliced
2 cloves garlic, minced
Hot buttered noodles
1 1/2 tbsp. parsley chopped
Salt
Pepper

How to make it:

1. Sauté mushrooms and onions in hot butter until golden brown, in a large skillet.
2. Remove from skillet and set aside. Add bacon to skillet and fry until crisp; remove with a slotted spoon and reserve.
3. Add Top Sirloin steak to skillet and fry in bacon fat, stirring frequently, until well browned.
4. Return mushroom and onion mixture to skillet and add flour; toss until flour disappears.
5. Add wine, bay leaf, garlic beef broth and thyme.
6. Simmer, covered, for 30 minutes, stirring frequently.

7. Add cooked bacon and carrot, and cook covered, for 15 minutes longer.
8. Season with salt and pepper. Before serving, remove bay leaf. Serve over hot buttered noodles. Sprinkle with parsley.

Bacon in Turkey Burger

Serves 6

Ingredients:

3 tbsp. sweet onion finely chopped
1-1/2 lbs. ground turkey
2 cloves garlic freshly minced
1/4 tsp. black pepper freshly ground
1/2 cup button mushrooms sliced thin
1 cup cheddar cheese shredded
1 green onion finely chopped
6 slices turkey bacon crisply cooked and crumbled
1/4 cup mayonnaise

How you make it:

1. Mix ground turkey, garlic, sweet onion, and pepper, in a bowl; combine well. Shape into 6 patties.
2. In another small bowl, mushrooms, combine cheese, green onion, cooked bacon, and mayonnaise; mix well.
3. Broil or grill burgers 4-6 inches from the flame, over medium temperature or coals for about 10-12 minutes, turning once.
4. During the last several minutes of cooking, spoon 1/4 cup cheese topping on each burger. Continue cooking until the cheese is melted.

Bacon and Cheese Puffs

These puffy little ham and cheese biscuits make a great snack or appetizer.

Serves 10

Ingredients:

2 tbsp. shredded Cheddar cheese
2 tbsp. Canadian bacon
7 1/2 oz. Refrigerator buttermilk biscuits or rolls -
1 package reduced-fat
3 tbsp. seasoned tomato sauce

How you make it:

1. Preheat the oven to 450 degrees.
2. Spray a small baking sheet with nonstick spray coating. Set aside.
3. Open the biscuit carton, and separate the biscuits.
4. Place them on the baking sheet.
5. With a small spoon, spread the tomato sauce on the biscuits, dividing the mixture evenly.
6. Top with the cheese and ham, dividing evenly.
7. Bake in the center of the oven for 8 to 10 minutes or until golden. Serve hot.
8. Leftovers will keep 1 to 2 days in the refrigerator, tightly wrapped.

McDonalds Quiche

Serves 6

Ingredients:

4 eggs
1 cup shredded natural Swiss cheese
1/2 pound of bacon, crisply fried and crumbled
1/3 cup minced red onion
2 cups whipping cream
1/8 tsp. cayenne pepper
1/4 tsp. equivalent of sweetener
1/4 tsp. salt

How you make it:

1. Heat oven to 425.
2. Sprinkle cheese, bacon and onion in the bottom of a 9-inch pie pan.
3. Beat eggs lightly and beat in remaining ingredients.
4. Pour cream mixture into pie pan.
5. Bake in oven for about 15 minutes.
6. Reduce oven temperature to 300 degrees and bake 30 minutes or longer or until a knife inserted 1 inch from the edge comes out clean.
7. Let stand 10 minutes before cutting. Serve in wedges.
8. This makes a soft-textured quiche. If a firmer texture is desired, cook for an additional 10 minutes.

Bacon Cheeseburger Quiche

Serves 6

Ingredients:

3 eggs
1 lb. very lean hamburger
4 slices crisp-cooked bacon, chopped in bits
1/2 cup mayonnaise
1 small chopped onion
1/2 cup half-n-half
Garlic powder to taste (optional)
White pepper
8 oz. shredded cheddar or Swiss cheese

How you make it:

1. Brown hamburger in skillet with onion.
2. Remove and mix in bowl with bacon pieces, breaking up any larger clumps with a fork or pastry mixer until you have a fine mix.
3. Drain well of any excess grease and press into the bottom of a deep-dish pie pan. Set aside.
4. Preheat oven to 350°F.
5. Mix the remaining ingredients in mixer bowl and whip well.
6. Pour mixture over beef "crust" and bake 40-45 minutes until top is browned and "set".
7. Cool 15-20 minutes before slicing.
8. This can be packaged in Ziplocs or plastic containers for meals quickly microwaved over the next 3-5 days.

Bacon and Leek Quiche

Serves 8

Ingredients:

Salt and freshly ground pepper
1 bunch fresh spinach, well rinsed and trimmed
1 teaspoon canola oil
2 ounces Canadian bacon, trimmed of fat and finely minced
2 pounds leeks, quartered, washed, and finely chopped
1 egg, lightly beaten
1 teaspoon Dijon mustard
2 ounces low-fat goat cheese
1/3 cup Parmesan shards
2 teaspoons unsalted butter
1/2 cup skim milk

How you make it:

1. Preheat the oven to 375 degrees F.
2. Lightly spray or wipe a 9-inch pie plate with vegetable oil.
3. Place the spinach leaves in a vegetable steamer over low heat and steam until just wilted, about 1 minute.
4. Line the pie plate with the spinach leaves.
5. Season with salt and freshly ground pepper to taste.
6. Heat the oil in a saucepan.
7. Add the leek, cover, and sweat for 5 minutes. Whisk the egg, skim milk, Canadian bacon, mustard, and goat cheese, and add the leek.
8. Pour the mixture carefully over the spinach, top with the Parmesan, and dot with the butter.
9. Bake for 45 minutes, or until set. Serve warm.

HOT BACON DRESSING

Serves 2

Ingredients:

2 tablespoons minced shallots
1/2 pound bacon slices
1 garlic clove, minced
1/4 cup cider vinegar
1/4 cup firmly packed brown sugar
1 teaspoon chopped fresh parsley
1/2 teaspoon pepper
Serve with spinach salad.
1/4 teaspoon salt

How you make it:
Mix all the Ingredients.

Bacon and Egg Quiche

Serves 2

Ingredients:
4 eggs
1 cup of heavy whipping creme
1 cup cheese
12 strips of bacon chopped fine
1/8 tsp. cayenne pepper
1/4 cup chopped onion
1/2 tsp. pepper
A little garlic, powder or fresh
1/4 tsp. salt

How you make it:

1.   Combine all the ingredients and dump into a lightly buttered 9 inches pie pan and bake at 425 for the first 15 minutes, then 300 for the next 30 minutes, remove let and let sit for 10 minutes.
2.   Serve immediately.

Bacon in Spinach Salad

For those of you who like spinach salad, you've got to try this. Its to die for. This recipe is for 2 large side dish salads. Very few carbs, I think.

Serves 2

Ingredients:

2 tablespoons wine vinegar
1/2 bag spinach, washed and torn into mouthful size pieces
1 teaspoon minced onion
4 slices bacon diced
1 tablespoon Splenda
1 teaspoon lemon juice
1 hard-boiled egg, coarsely chopped.
1 tablespoon oil
Some freshly ground pepper
1/2 teaspoon salt
4 large mushrooms, sliced

How you make it:

1. Put the spinach in a bowl and set aside.
2. Then fry the bacon and minced onion in a skillet until the bacon is crispy.
3. Add lemon juice, vinegar, oil, splenda, salt and pepper and just mix together.
4. Pour over spinach and toss until the leaves are well coated.
5. Add the mushrooms and egg and toss a little more.
6. Serve immediately. Enjoy!

Bacon in Toscana Soup

Serves 2

Ingredients:

4 oz. cream cheese
1 lb. ground sausage
16 oz. bag of frozen cauliflower (use fresh if you want)
1 onion
1 cup heavy whipping cream
3 tbsp. butter
1 cup Kale
Garlic, salt, pepper to taste
4 cups water

How you make it:

1. Microwave or steam cauliflower until soft, for about 10 minutes.
2. While cauliflower is softening, cook bacon, sausage, and onion together until done, drain well.
3. Mash cauliflower together with butter and cream cheese.
4. Put water and kale in soup pot and cook for about 2 minutes.
5. Add the cauliflower mixture, meat and seasonings.
6. Simmer until kale has your desired tenderness, for about 5-10 minutes.

CHEESE AND BUTTER

BUTTER is the fatty constituent of milk. It is obtained by skimming or separating the cream from milk and churning it in order to make the particles of fat adhere to one another. Butter is used largely in the household as an article of food, for it is one of the most appetizing and digestible forms of fat.

The flavor of butter depends to a great extent on the kind of cream from which it is made, both sweet and sour cream being used for this purpose. Of these two kinds, sour cream is the preferable one, because it gives to the butter a desirable flavor. Still, the unsalted butter that is made from sweet cream is apparently growing in favor, although it is usually more
expensive than salted butter. The difference in price is due to the fact that unsalted butter spoils readily.

CHEESE

Cheese is a product that is manufactured from the solids of milk, and it provides a valuable food. The making of cheese was known in ancient times, it having probably originated through a desire to utilize an oversupply of milk.

Cheese offers a valuable source of nutriment for the body, because its food value ranks high. The food value in 1 pound of cheese is equivalent to that in 2 pounds of beef, that in 24 eggs, or that in 4 pounds of fish. The use of cheese, however, is not nearly so great as its food value warrants, the amount used in the United States per capita being only about 3-1/2 pounds annually. This is a condition that should be overcome, for there is a large variety of ways in which cheese can be used to advantage in the diet. When eaten raw, it is very appetizing, and when used with soups, sauces, and foods that have a bland taste, it lends additional flavor and makes an especially attractive dish. In addition, the fact that it is an economical food and can be conveniently kept and stored should recommend its frequent use.

Below are delicious Foods You can Prepare with this Healthy Fats:

Almond Butter Sponge cake

Serves: 1

Ingredients:

1 tbsp. Coconut Milk
1 oz. almond butter 1.2
1 egg, separated
1/8 tsp. stevia powder
1/2 tsp. vanilla extract

How you make it:

1.   To make smooth batter, combine egg yolk with all the other ingredients.
2.   Whip egg white until stiff. Get your batter and carefully fold whipped egg white into.
3.   Pour into small medium sized loaf pan lined with baking paper.
4.   For 25 minutes you bake at low temp.

Buttery Cheesecake Bites

Servings: 100 appetizer bites

Ingredients:
4 teaspoons butter
1 pound cream cheese
2 eggs

How you make it:

1. Preheat oven to 325°.
2. Melt butter in 9-inch glass baking dish.
3. Beat together eggs and cream cheese. Pour into baking dish.
4. Bake at 325° for 20 minutes, until puffy and brown.
5. Chill thoroughly. Cut into 3/4 inch squares and set out as an appetizer with toothpicks.

Crustless Breakfast Quiche

Serves 4

Ingredients:

1 1/2 cups Heavy cream
1 teaspoon Butter
1 cup Cheddar cheese -- grated
2 teaspoons onion – chopped
2 teaspoons dried basil
3/4 teaspoon paprika
1/4 teaspoon garlic powder
Salt and pepper
4 each eggs

How you make it:

1. Preheat oven to 325.
2. Rub coconut oil at the bottom and sides of a 9-inch pie pan.
3. Add cream to a medium saucepan and heat until scalded.
4. Reduce heat and stir in grated cheese.
5. When cheese is melted, onion, paprika, add basil, and garlic powder.
6. Remove from heat and cool for about 5 minutes.
7. Then add one egg at a time and mix in thoroughly until all eggs are used.
8. Salt and pepper to taste, and mix well. Pour mixture into pie pan, place in oven, and bake until custard is set (45-50 minutes). Serve hot or cold.

Pepperoni Frittata

Makes 6 servings

Ingredients:

6 eggs

1/4 lb. pepperoni slices
1/2 C Parmesan cheese, grated
4 oz. mozzarella cheese, shredded
1 med. onion, sliced
1/2 C mushrooms, sliced
2 tsp. butter
1 C broccoli, chopped
1 med. green pepper

How you make it:

1. Place butter in frying pan. Add mushrooms, onion, green peppers pepperoni, and broccoli.
2. Sauté' until onion is almost done, for about 3 to 4 minutes.
3. Beat eggs with Parmesan cheese.
4. Pour over vegetables in frying pan. Do not cover.
5. Let cook until eggs are just about cooked, then sprinkle with Mozzarella cheese.
6. Cook until cheese melts and serve.

Cheese Puffs

Makes 8 Servings

Ingredients:

1 stick butter
1 pkg. (3 oz.) cream cheese
1/4 lb. sharp cheddar cheese
Pork Rinds
2 egg whites, stiffly beaten

How you make it:

1. Melt cheddar cheese, cream cheese, and margarine in a double boiler.
2. Fold cheese mixture into stiff egg whites. Dip pork rinds.
3. Let stand in refrigerator overnight Bake the puffs in a slow oven, 250 degrees, or until crisp, for about an hour.
4. The texture comes out like a cookie.

Cheese With Baked Cod

4 Servings, about 3 ounces each

Ingredients:

Cheddar cheese, shredded 4 tablespoons
Cod fillets, fresh or frozen 1 pound

How you make it:

1. Thaw cod according to package directions.
2. Prepare cod according to package directions.
3. After cod is fully cooked, sprinkle cheese on cod.
4. Return cod to oven to melt cheese, about 3 to 5 minutes.

Stuffed Mozzarella

Serves 4

Ingredients:

3/4 pound fresh spinach – steamed
4 ounces mozzarella cheese
2 red bell peppers - sliced lengthwise
2 cups mixed salad greens
1 tablespoon balsamic vinegar
2 tomatoes – sliced

How you make it:

1.   Flatten fresh mozzarella to 1/2" width.
2.   Layer with spinach and red peppers.
3.   Roll up jellyroll fashion from longest end.
4.   Slice and serve with greens, tomatoes slices drizzled with balsamic vinegar.

Delicious Cheese cube

Serves 6

Ingredients:

1 tablespoon butter
8 whole eggs, separated
1/4 teaspoon ground black pepper
1/2 teaspoon salt
2 ounces cheddar cheese, grated finely

How you make it:

1. Heat oven to 400°.
2. Beat egg whites until soft peaks form.
3. Do not over beat, or your soufflé will be dry.
4. Beat egg yolks. Continue beating at high speed, in another bowl.
5. Meanwhile, melt butter in a 9-inch square glass baking pan.
6. Beat salt and pepper into egg yolks.
7. Stir half of the cheese into egg yolks, with a fork.
8. Then fold in the whites.
9. With the back of a spoon, remove the hot pan from oven and spread the butter around.
10. Pour soufflé mixture into the pan.
11. Sprinkle the soufflé with the other half of the cheese.
12. Return the pan to oven. Bake 15 - 20 minutes, until nicely browned.
13. Cut into squares. Serve immediately.

Cottage Cheese Pie

Serve 2

Ingredients:

1 cup sugar
4 eggs
4 teaspoons vanilla
1 can pet milk (or any evaporated milk)
2 tablespoons flour
1 Lb. Cottage Cheese
Nutmeg

How you make it:

1. Beat first six ingredients well in a Blender.
2. Pour into 2 unbaked pie shells and sprinkle nutmeg over the tops.
3. Bake in a very slow (250 degrees) oven for about one hour. Cottage

Crab-Cheese Dip

Serve 2

Ingredients:

1 container (8 oz.) creamed cottage cheese
2 cans (6 1/2 oz. each) crab meat
2 tbsp. mayonnaise
1 tbsp. lemon juice
1 tbsp. prepared mustard
1/2 tsp. salt
Twisted lemon slices
Parsley

How you make it:

1. Drain crab meat thoroughly.
2. Reserve reddest pieces for garnish.
3. Put remaining half in container of electric blender with mayonnaise, cheese, and mustard, lemon juice and salt.
4. Whirl until blended. Place in bowl and garnish with remaining parsley, lemon slices crab meat.

Bacon Cheesecake Bites

This meal is very healthy and good if you are expecting Some Guest

Servings: 64 appetizer bites

Ingredients:

2 eggs
4 teaspoons butter
1 pound bacon
1 pound cream cheese

How you make it:

1.   Preheat oven to 325°.
2.   Melt butter in 9 inch glass baking dish.
3.   Beat together cream cheese and eggs. Pour into baking dish. Bake at 325° for 20 minutes, until puffy and brown.
4.   Chill thoroughly. Cut into 1-inch squares.
5.   Cut bacon in thirds, making 6 small strips out of each strip of bacon.
6.   Fry until bacon is somewhat limp. You want to be able to bend it, but you don't want it too limp.
7.   Wrap the perimeter of each Cheesecake Bite in a bacon strip. Arrange on a cookie sheet. Broil until bacon is crisp for about 1-2 minutes. Serve hot.

(Note: your guests will probably eat 4-5 each, depending on the total amount of food you are serving.)

McDonalds Chicken Cheese Dip

Makes for 6

Ingredients:

3/4 cup mayonnaise
2 cups chopped, cooked chicken
2 green onions, minced
1/4 tsp. dried thyme
1/2 tsp. dried basil
1/2 tsp. salt
1/2 cup grated Swiss cheese
1/4 tsp. pepper
1/2 cup grated Parmesan cheese

How you make it:

1. Preheat oven to 350°.
2. Combine together mayonnaise, chicken, green onions, spices, Swiss cheese and 2 tablespoons Parmesan cheese.
3. Put mixture in a buttered casserole dish. Sprinkle the rest of the Parmesan cheese on top. Bake about 10 minutes, until top is browned.

John's Cheese Ball

Ingredients:

2-3 green onions (chopped)
16 oz. cream cheese (softened)
3/4 tsp. mustard
1/2 tsp. cayenne pepper
1 tbsp. mayonnaise
1 tsp. paprika
1 tsp. garlic powder
1 tsp. Accent
1 tsp. Worcestershire sauce
1/2 cup chopped pecans
1 tsp. Tabasco sauce (optional)

How you make it:

1. Mix all ingredients except the pecans, and shape into a ball.
2. Roll ball in pecans, and enjoy!!!

Quiche with Swiss cheese

Serves 6

Ingredients:

4 large eggs
4 oz. cream cheese, softened
1 1/4 cups heavy cream
1/4 tsp. black pepper
1/8 tsp. cayenne pepper (optional)
1/2 tsp. salt
1 1/4 tsp. garlic powder
4 oz. grated Swiss cheese
1 medium sweet red pepper, sliced in about 1/4" strips
13 oz. canned flaked ham (2 cans)

How you make it:

1. Preheat oven to 350 F.
2. Add eggs, cream cheese, heavy cream, salt, black pepper, garlic powder, cayenne pepper, and mix well, in a medium size mixing bowl.
3. Adjust seasonings to taste at this point.
4. Layer grated Swiss cheese, flaked ham and half of the sliced red pepper strips in bottom of pie dish.
5. Pour the egg mixture on top.
6. Top the remaining sliced red pepper strips around the pie, placing strips from the center to outside.
7. Bake in preheated 350 F oven for 50 to 55 minutes.
8. Test if its done, by sticking a wood tester or toothpick into center, if done, should come out dry.
9. Let it stand for 15 minutes before cutting and serving.

Seductive Seafood Quiche

Serves 6

Ingredients:

4 eggs
1 1/2 cups shredded Swiss cheese
1/2 cup green onion slices
8 oz. crab flakes (use real crab)
1/2 teaspoon salt
Dash of pepper
1 1/4 cups heavy cream

How you make it:

1. Preheat oven to 350 degrees F.
2. Sprinkle cheese, onion, crab, and seasonings in pie plate.
3. Beat together eggs and heavy cream.
4. Pour over cheese mixture.
5. Bake 55 to 60 min or until set. Can substitute sharp cheddar for Swiss cheese.

Creamy Cheesecake

Makes 8 servings

Ingredients:

2 eggs
Cracker crust (6 oz. or 9 inch)
1 lbs. Crème cheese softened
1/2 cup sugar
1 ready to use graham
1/2 tsp. Vanilla

How you make it:

1. Mix sugar, Crème cheese, and vanilla with electric mixer on medium speed until well blended.
2. Pour into crust.
3. Bake at 350 f for about 40 min. Or until center is almost set. Cool.
4. Refrigerate 3 hrs. or overnight. Enjoy!

Sprouts weds Cheddar

Serves 4

Ingredients:

1 pound fresh Brussels sprouts
1/4 teaspoon dry mustard
4 ounces cheddar cheese, shredded
1 tablespoon water
¼ teaspoon ground black pepper
1 egg yolk

How you make it:

1. Steam Brussels sprouts; drain. Arrange in nice serving dish.
2. Melt water and cheddar cheese in microwave.
3. Stir in mustard and ground black pepper.
4. Beat egg yolk. Add to cheese mixture, stirring constantly with fork or wire whisk.
5. Microwave until bubbly but not boiling, for about half a minute.
6. Stir; pour sauce over Brussels sprouts.

Orange Cheesecake

Serves 8

Ingredients:

1 cup of cream
Zest of one orange
1 pound of cream cheese (softened)
1/2 - 2/3 cup of Splenda (depends on how sweet you want it)
4 tablespoons of vanilla
4 eggs
1/4 teaspoon of salt

How you make it:

1. Preheat oven to 350 degrees.
2. Mix all ingredients together with a mixer until completely smooth.
3. Pour into a 10-inch pie plate (preferably glass).
4. Bake at 350 for 25 minutes.
5. Then turn heat down to 300 degrees and bake for 15 – 20 minutes more or until a knife inserted in the center comes out clean.
6. What I like to do is turn the oven off completely for the last five minutes, and leave the cake inside.
7. Then take the cheesecake out and leave on counter until room temperature. Then chill.

Cheese N Yoghurt

Ingredients:

1 quart milk
1 tablespoon plain yogurt
1 cup heavy cream

How you make it:

1. Combine milk and cream and bring to a boil.
2. Let cool down to about 70F, then stir in the yogurt.
3. Keep at 110 degrees for 8 hours. One cup is 4grams of carbohydrate

D' Best Cheesed Asparagus

Serves 8

Ingredients:

2 pounds Asparagus
2 cups shredded mozzarella cheese
1/2 teaspoon olive oil
8 ounces brie, sliced
1/4 teaspoon ground cayenne pepper
2 cups shredded mild cheddar cheese, shredded

How you make it:

1. Wash Asparagus trim and discard woody ends.
2. Steam Asparagus 3 minutes.
3. Grease a 9-inch glass baking dish with olive or coconut oil. Lay asparagus in pan. Arrange brie slices over asparagus.
4. Sprinkle cheddar cheese over brie, and mozzarella cheese over all.
5. Sprinkle with ground cayenne pepper.
6. Bake at 350° for 15 to 20 minutes, until cheeses are melted but not bubbling.

Strawberry Cheesecake

Serves 6-8

Ingredients:

8 oz. Cream cheese,
4 oz. heavy cream,
4 packets Sweet 'n Low or Canadian Splenda,
2 Eggs
2 tsp. Vanilla extract
1 cup sliced Strawberries,
1/2 cup Sour Cream

How you make it:

1. Preheat oven to 350 degrees.
2. Combine cream cheese, heavy cream, 3 packets of Sweet N Low or Canadian Splenda, eggs and vanilla extract, In a blender or food processor.
3. Blend until completely smooth.
4. Pour into an 8" ceramic or Pyrex pie pan.
5. Bake for 25 minutes.
6. Chill well. Garnish with sliced strawberries and sour cream

Sumptuous Rarebit

Serves 8

Ingredients:

1/4 cup heavy cream
1 tablespoon butter
2 cups cheddar cheese, grated
1/2 teaspoon dry mustard
2 egg yolks
1/4 teaspoon black pepper

How you make it:

1. Melt cheese and butter in double boiler or microwave, stirring until smooth.
2. Add mustard and pepper. Stir well.
3. Combine egg yolks and cream in a small bowl.
4. Beat with a fork until thoroughly mixed.
5. Slowly add to cheese mixture. Serve over fish fillets, chicken, or vegetables.
6. Excellent as a hot dip with raw vegetables.

Cheesy Spinach Casserole

Ingredients:

3 oz. cream cheese
2 10-oz. packages frozen chopped spinach
1/2 c. pecans, chopped (walnuts work well too)
Salt and pepper
1/4 c. butter

How you make it:

1. Cook spinach in salted water. Drain.
2. Melt cream cheese and butter together and add to spinach.
3. Put in casserole dish. Top with Parmesan and pecans. Heat at 350 degrees. About 4 servings.

EGGs AND MILK

Milk As is well understood, milk is the liquid that is secreted by the mammary glands of female mammals for the nourishment of their young. The word milk as it is commonly used, however, refers to cow's milk, because such milk is employed to a greater extent as human food than the milk from any other animal.

Nevertheless, Because of the double usefulness of protein-to serve as fuel and to make and repair muscular tissue-this element is regarded as an important ingredient of milk. The protein in milk is called casein.

The other substance in milk that serves as fuel, or to produce energy, is fat. It occurs in the form of tiny particles, each surrounded by a thin covering and suspended in the liquid. Such a mixture, which is called an emulsion, is the most easily digested form in which fat is found.

Like milk, eggs are often spoken of as a perfect food. Still, as has been pointed out, they are not a perfect food for man, but they are of especial nutritive value and should be used freely in the diet just as long as their cost neither limits nor prohibits their use.

Studies shows that eggs contain proportionately almost as much fat as protein and that nearly all this fat is found in the yolk. Since fat produces more heat or energy, weight for weight, than any other food substance, and since eggs contain neither starch nor sugar, it is evident that the fat of this food is the main source of the energy-producing material.

Now on The Recipes Using Eggs and Milk:

McDonalds Devilled Eggs

Serves 12

Ingredients:

1/2 cup sour cream
6 hard-cooked eggs
1/2 cup flaked canned salmon
2 teaspoons prepared mustard
2 teaspoons lemon juice
1/8 teaspoon curry powder
1-1/2 teaspoons Worcestershire sauce
Paprika
Salt, pepper

How you make it:

1. Shell eggs, then cut in halves length ways and remove yolks.
2. Mash yolks and mix with salmon, sour cream, curry powder, lemon juice, mustard, and Worcestershire and season to taste with salt and pepper.
3. Pile mixture into whites and garnish with Paprika.
4. Makes 12 halves.

Eggs Fritata

Serves 1

Ingredients:

2 eggs
2 cups fresh spinach
1/2 teaspoon olive oil
1 clove garlic, grated

How you make it:

1. Wash spinach thoroughly in warm salt water. Rinse.
2. Remove stems. Chop coarsely. Cook spinach until it wilts.
3. Beat in eggs and garlic. In medium saucepan, heat olive oil.
4. Pour in egg mixture. Cook until egg is firm, about a minute or two on each side.

Southern Scotch Eggs

Makes 6

Ingredients:

2 large eggs
12 ounces pork breakfast sausage, ground
1/2 teaspoon coarse salt
6 hard-boiled eggs, peeled
1/4 teaspoon freshly ground pepper
3 tablespoons Soy flour
1 teaspoon chopped fresh sage
1 tablespoon chopped flat-leaf parsley
1/4 teaspoon freshly grated nutmeg
1 cup Wheat gem

How you make it:

1. Heat oven to 400 degrees. In a medium bowl, combine sausage, one uncooked egg, salt, and pepper. Form into six patties of equal size. Mold each patty around one hard-boiled egg.

2. Place gluten or soy flour in a bowl, and set aside. Lightly whisk remaining uncooked egg in a second bowl, and set aside. In a third bowl, combine parsley, sage, nutmeg, gluten and pork rind crumbs.

3. Roll each sausage-covered egg in the gluten or soy flour, coating it, and shake off any excess. Dip the coated egg in the bowl with the whisked egg, coating it, then roll in the herb- crumb mixture to cover completely.

4. Place eggs on the baking sheet. Bake until dark golden brown, 30 to 35 minutes, rotating the eggs several times for an even golden brown color.

Southwestern Swiss Eggs

Serves 8

Ingredients:

8 eggs

2 tablespoons butter

1/4 pound Swiss cheese, grated

1/3 cup light cream

1/4 teaspoon ground black pepper

1/4 teaspoon salt

1/2 teaspoon dry mustard

How you make it:

1. Sprinkle cheese on bottom of a greased 2 quart baking dish.

2. Dot with butter. Mix cream with pepper, salt, and mustard.

3. Pour half over the cheese.

4. Beat eggs. Pour eggs into pan.

5. Pour remaining cream mixture over eggs.

6. Bake at 325° until eggs are set, or for about 30 minutes.

Cloud 9 Omelet

Serves 2

Ingredients:

1 tablespoon butter

4 eggs

1/2 teaspoon salt

1/4 teaspoon ground black pepper

1/4 cup water

How you make it:

1. In a bowl, Beat eggs, water, salt, and pepper thoroughly.

2. Melt butter in medium skillet, buttering sides of pan.

3. Turn heat to medium, after pouring eggs into skillet.

4. Cook until edges begin to look set.

5. Lift edges of omelet as they begin to set, allowing uncooked egg to flow under the omelet.

6. When omelet is set but still moist, turn heat up and brown bottom. Fold omelet. Slide onto warm plate.

7. Enjoy!

Sea Breeze Scrambled Eggs

Serves 4

Ingredients:

1/2 teaspoon dried tarragon
2 tablespoons milk
2 tablespoons butter
4 eggs
4 ounces imitation crab meat (shredded)
3 ounces cream cheese (cut in pieces)
Salt and pepper to taste

How you make it:

1. Mix eggs with tarragon, milk, salt and pepper.
2. Melt butter over medium high heat, in a skillet.
3. Add crab and warm while stirring.
4. Add egg mixture and scramble until about 80% done.
5. Stir in cream cheese and continue cooking until eggs are set and cream cheese is melted.

Egg Drop Soup

Serves 4

Ingredients:

1 teaspoon salt
2 eggs
2 teaspoons finely chopped scallions
2 cups chicken broth

How you make it:

1. Beat eggs with a bit of the salt. Set aside.
2. Bring chicken broth to boil. Stir in remaining salt.
3. Slowly pour the beaten eggs into the boiling broth, stirring constantly.
4. Cook one minute.
5. Pour soup into serving bowls. Sprinkle with scallions.

Eggs Florentine

Ingredients:

1 pkg. frozen, chopped spinach
1 lb. creamed cottage cheese
6 large eggs
1/2 lb. Feta cheese
1/2 lb. grated Swiss cheese
Nutmeg
1/4 lb. butter or margarine
Dash hot pepper sauce

How you make it:

1. Beat eggs.
2. Add cheeses and butter and mix well.
3. Cook and drain spinach well.
4. Add to egg/cheese mixture.
5. Add nutmeg and hot pepper sauce.
6. Pour into greased 3 quart baking dish and bake @ 350 degrees for 40 minutes. Cut into squares.

Egg with Mushroom Soufflés

Serves 6

Ingredients:

4 eggs, separated
2/3 cup heavy cream
3 tablespoons butter
1/2 teaspoon salt
1 cup grated cheddar cheese
1/2 pound mushrooms, sliced
1/4 teaspoon ground black pepper

How you make it:

1. Heat oven to 375°.
2. Set a pan of water on bottom rack of oven.
3. Melt 2 tablespoons butter over low heat.
4. Stir in salt, cream, and pepper.
5. Add cheese, and stir until sauce is thick.
6. Beat egg yolks in medium bowl for 5 minutes using an electric mixer.
7. Add slowly to cheese mixture.
8. Take off the cheese mixture from heat and allow to cool.
9. Sauté mushrooms in remaining butter.
10. Arrange mushrooms in lightly greased 1 1/2 quart baking dish.
11. When cheese mixture is thoroughly cooled, beat egg whites until stiff, with electric mixer, using clean bowl and beaters.
12. Do not over beat. Fold egg whites into cheese mixture.
13. Spoon mixture over mushrooms. Bake at 375° for 30 minutes. Serve immediately.

Egg Custard

Serves 2

Ingredients:

1 egg
1/2 c. cream mixed with 1/2 cup water
1 egg yolk
3 tbsp. sugar substitute (Splenda)
1/8 tsp. salt
1 tsp. vanilla extract
1/8 tsp. ground nutmeg

Ingredients:

1. Beat the egg and yolk lightly.
2. Add Splenda, cream, vanilla and salt.
3. Pour into two ungreased 6 ounce custard cups.
4. Sprinkle with nutmeg. Set in a pan containing 1/2 to 1 inch of hot water.
5. Bake at 350 degrees until set, or for about 35 minutes.

Ecstatic Egg Salad

Serves 4

Ingredients:

1/4 cup finely chopped celery
8 hard-boiled eggs, chopped
4 large lettuce leaves
1/4 cup finely chopped dill pickle
1 scallion, finely chopped1/3 cup mayonnaise
Dash pepper
1 teaspoon chopped fresh parsley
1/4 teaspoon salt

How you make it:

1. Mix all ingredients except lettuce leaves and parsley.
2. Chill. Just prior to serving, Pile on lettuce leaves. Sprinkle with parsley.

Tasty Broccoli with Eggs

Serves 6

Ingredients:

1/2 pound bacon

10 ounce package frozen broccoli

¾ cup grated Swiss cheese

3 eggs, beaten

1 bunch scallions, finely chopped

¾ cup heavy cream

1/4 teaspoon ground black pepper

1/2 teaspoon salt

How you make it:

1.   Preheat oven to 400°.

2.   Cook broccoli following the package directions. Drain.

3.   Cook bacon until crisp. Remove from pan.

4.   Sauté scallions in bacon fat for one minute.

5.   Arrange scallions, bacon, and broccoli in 9-inch pie pan.

6.   Sprinkle cheese over broccoli. Combine cream, eggs, salt, and pepper.

7.   Pour over broccoli. Bake for about 15 minutes.

8.   Reduce heat to 325° and continue baking, until knife inserted near center comes out clean, for about 20 more minutes.

9.   Serve Immediately.

Italian Pie

Serves 4

Ingredients:

1 10-ounce package frozen chopped spinach

1 bunch scallions, chopped

3 eggs

8 ounces Feta cheese

1 cup whole milk ricotta cheese

1/4 teaspoon salt

1/4 teaspoon ground black pepper

How you make it:

1. Preheat oven to 425°.

2. Cook spinach according to package directions.

3. Drain thoroughly, squeezing out as much water as possible.

4. Spread spinach in buttered 9-inch pie pan.

5. Beat eggs in medium bowl. Stir in scallions, salt, cheeses and pepper.

6. Pour carefully over spinach. Bake 30 minutes until set. Cool 10 minutes before serving.

Ultimate Egg Omelet

Serves 1

Ingredients:

2 cups sliced fresh mushrooms

2 eggs

1 teaspoon olive oil

2 tablespoons grated cheddar cheese

1 tablespoon chopped scallions

How you make it:

1. Sauté mushrooms in a little olive oil until almost ready to give up their liquid.

2. Remove from pan and set aside. Beat eggs.

3. Pour into same pan and cook over medium heat until partly solid.

4. Sprinkle with cheese, scallions, and half of the mushrooms.

5. Fold over and continue cooking until hot. Top with rest of mushrooms.

Spinach Cheese Pie

Serves 8

Ingredients:

2 TB butter
2 (10 oz.) packages frozen whole-leaf spinach, defrosted (I use chopped spinach)
1 bunch scallions, including the firm green, chopped (about 3/4 c)
6 eggs, beaten well
1 (15 oz.) container whole-milk ricotta
1/2 medium onion, chopped
1/2 pound feta cheese, crumbled
1 TB chopped dill
1/4 c chopped parsley
Salt and pepper to taste
Olive oil for the pan
Pinch of grated nutmeg

How you make it:

1. Preheat the oven to 350F.
2. Let the spinach drain in a colander in the sink.
3. To get all the excess moisture out of the spinach, the easiest way is to line your hand with a double thickness of paper towels and squeeze handfuls of spinach dry.
4. Then chop it and set aside.
5. Melt the butter in a large skillet; when it's foaming, add the scallions and chopped onion.
6. Cook them over medium heat until they're soft, then add the spinach and a sprinkle of salt and pepper, and cook for 3 minutes, stirring from time to time.
7. Beat the eggs in a large mixing bowls and whisk in the ricotta.
8. Stir in the remaining ingredients, and then oil a 13x9-inch baking dish well with coconut or Olive oil, including the sides.
9. Mix the spinach with the egg-cheese mixture, taste for seasoning, and pour into the pan.

10. Bake the pie for 30 to 40 minutes, until the moisture disappears and the top has dappled golden spots.
11. Remove from the oven and let sit for 5 minutes before serving.

Tasty Chicken Egg Foo Young

Serves 4

Ingredients:

1 cup shredded string beans
8 eggs
I cup sliced mushrooms, canned or fresh
I cup shredded celery
1 1/2 cups shredded cooked chicken
Salt and pepper to taste
1 cup shredded onions

How you make it:

1.   Place all ingredients in a mixing bowl, combine them thoroughly and divide into 8 portions.
2.   Grease well a hot skillet; fry both sides until golden brown.

POULTRY AND MEAT

POULTRY

POULTRY is the term used to designate birds that have been domesticated, or brought under the control of man, for two purposes, namely, the eggs they produce and the flesh food they supply. All the common species of domestic fowls-chickens, ducks, geese, turkeys, guinea fowls, and pigeons-are known as poultry.

MEAT

All meat, no matter how lean it appears, contains some fat. Meats that are very fat are higher in nutritive value than meats that contain only a small amount of this substance. Fat is a valuable constituent of food, for it is the most concentrated form in which the fuel elements of food are found. In supplying the body with fuel, it serves to maintain the body temperature and to yield energy in the form of muscular and other power.

Since this is such a valuable food material, it is important that the best possible use be made of all drippings and left-over fats and that not even the smallest amount of any kind be wasted.

Now, Let get started with these Delicious Recipes:

Smoked Chicken Wrapped in Bacon

Serves 4

Ingredients:

3 Tbsp. butter
4 boneless chicken breasts
1/2 tsp. garlic powder
1/4 tsp. cayenne
1/4 tsp. paprika
1/2 cup smoked Gouda cheese
1/2 tsp. black pepper
4 slices bacon
Salt

How you make it:

1. Preheat oven to 350 degrees. Flatten each chicken breast to 1/4 inch thickness.
2. Combine pepper, paprika, garlic powder, and the cayenne together in a small bowl and spread evenly on both sides of the chicken breasts.
3. Salt to taste.
4. Cut the smoked Gouda into small pieces and place ¼ of the cheese on each breast.
5. Starting with the narrow end Press down firmly and roll the breast.
6. Wrap each chicken breast with one piece of bacon.
7. Over medium heat, melt the butter in a skillet.
8. Brown the chicken rolls evenly in the butter until the bacon begins to crisp.
9. Place the four chicken rolls in a baking dish and bake at 350 degrees for 20 minutes. Serve immediately.

Melodious Meatloaf

Serves 4

Ingredients:

1 egg
1 lb. ground chuck
1/2 cup heavy cream
1 cup pork rinds
2 tbsp. Worcestershire sauce
Salt to taste
3/4 cup shredded cheese

How you make it:

1. Crunch the pork rinds up into crumbs.
2. Put the meat in a microwave-safe baking dish.
3. Add the Worcestershire sauce, pork rind crumbs, egg, cream, and cheese.
4. Add salt to taste.
5. Stir until all ingredients are mixed thoroughly and shape into a loaf.
6. Put into microwave and cook until internal temp rises to 150, or for about 14 minutes.

McDonalds Skillet Meatloaf

Serves 4

Ingredients:

1 garlic clove minced
2 1/2 lb. ground beef
1 small onion grated
1 Tbsp. catsup
1 egg
Salt and pepper

Sauce:
1 can of tomato puree
Several fresh basil leaves chopped
1 tsp. sugars (omit or substitute with sweetener)
1 small can of mushroom pieces drained
Worcestershire sauce
1 large onion sliced

How you make it:

1. Make meatloaf mixture by combining onion, meat, egg and seasoning.
2. Form into a round loaf.
3. Heat some olive oil in a heavy-duty skillet.
4. Pat meat into pan and brown on both sides; carefully turning with wide spatula.
5. Mix tomato paste, an empty paste can of water, sugar and basil and pour over meatloaf.
6. Add mushrooms and sliced onion to pan.
7. Sprinkle with a few splashes of Worcestershire sauce.
8. Cook covered over low heat for 1+ hour or until meatloaf is tender.
9. Occasionally stir sauce in pan and baste top of meatloaf.
10. Serve meatloaf with some of the thickened sauce.

The Ultimate Golumpki Casserole

Cabbage rolls without the rolls!!

Serves 5

Ingredients:

2 Eggs
1/2 lb. Ground pork or sausage
2 lb. Ground Round or chuck
4 Tbsp. Salt pork
2 large onions
1 large head of cabbage
3 cloves of garlic
3 large ripe tomatoes sliced thin
12 Mushrooms
3 strips of bacon
6 oz. V8 juice or tomato juice

How you make it:

1. Cut the core out of the cabbage and put in boiling water for 15 minutes.
2. Remove from pot and cool.
3. Put diced salt pork in fry pan and add diced garlic, chopped onions, and sliced mushrooms, cook until lightly browned.
4. In a bowl add pork, beef, eggs, onion mixture and mix or combine them well.
5. In a Dutch Oven pan cover the bottom with some of the tomatoes.
6. Remove the leaves from the head of cabbage and place a single layer in the pot.
7. Crumble the meat mixture between your fingers and drop onto cabbage leaves.
8. Spoon on some of the tomato juice and then put some slices of tomato, you can also put thin slices of onion if you wish.
9. Place another layer of cabbage leaves on top of this layer and repeat the process ending with a layer of cabbage leaves.

10. Place the uncooked bacon on top of the cabbage and cover.
11. Place into a preheated 325 degree oven for two and half hours.
12. Use the V8 juice to baste the casserole with to keep the top layer of cabbage moist.
13. Remove and let set for 20 minutes before serving.
14. Cut into serving pieces and serve.

Delicious Beef Tenderloin with cheese

Serves 4

Ingredients:

4 beef tenderloins

Sauce Ingredients:
1 cup Beef Stock or prepared Beef or Chicken Broth
2 cups Dry Red Wine
1/4 cup Shallots, finely chopped
1/2 stick of chilled Butter, cut into pieces
2 tsp. fresh Thyme, chopped

Cream Cheese Filling:
4 (6 to 8-oz.) Tenderloin Steaks, cut about 1 1/2-inch thick
2 (8-oz.) packages Cream Cheese, warmed to room temperature
1 tsp. fresh Thyme, chopped or 1/4 tsp. dried
1 tsp. Garlic, minced
1 tsp. Green Onion or Chives, thinly sliced or chopped
1 tsp. fresh Basil, chopped
1 tsp. fresh Tarragon, chopped or 1/4 tsp. dried
2 Tbsp. Olive Oil
Salt and Black Pepper to season

How you make it in 20 Easy Steps:

1. To prepare the sauce, combine the beef stock, dry red wine, shallots, and thyme in a heavy medium-sized saucepan over high heat.
2. Gently boil for about 30 minutes until reduced to 1/2 cup.
3. To prepare the tenderloin steaks, mix the garlic, cream cheese, tarragon, green onions, thyme or chives, and basil in a small bowl.
4. Season with salt and pepper.
5. It's important to note that both the sauce and cheese mixture can be prepared ahead of cooking the steaks.
6. Preheat the oven to 400-F degrees.
7. Using a small sharp knife, cut an X in the top center of each steak, making sure to cut 3/4 of the way through the steaks.

8.   Fill each X with 1 tablespoon of the cream cheese mixture.
9.   Season steaks with salt and pepper.
10. Warm the olive oil in heavy skillet over high heat.
11. Add steaks and cook with cut sides down until browned, about one minute.
12. Using a metal spatula, carefully turn steaks over, scraping up cheese crust along with steak.
13. Cook until bottom is brown, about another minute.
14. Transfer the heavy skillet to oven and cook steaks to desired doneness, about 12 minutes for rare.
15. Transfer steaks to serving plates.
16. Tent with foil to keep warm.
17. Bring sauce to simmer. Remove from heat.
18. Gradually add butter, whisking just until melted.
19. Season sauce with salt and pepper.
20. Spoon the warm sauce over the steaks and serve.

Pepperoni Pizza

Serves 2

Ingredients:

2 tbsp. Worcestershire sauce
1 lb. ground beef
1 tsp. garlic powder
1/4 cup pizza sauce
Pepperoni slices
Salt and pepper to taste
Red pepper strips
2 cups shredded mozzarella cheese
Sliced mushrooms

How you make it:

1. Mix ground beef, sliced mushroom, Worcestershire sauce and garlic powder and pat thinly in a pizza tray, bringing the meat mixture as close to the edge as possible (the "crust" will shrink during cooking).
2. Cook at 325 for 30 minutes. Remove from oven and drain all liquids from tray.
3. Pat top of "crust" with paper towels, removing as much of the juices as possible.
4. Spread the pizza sauce over top of "crust". Top with red pepper strips, pepperoni slices, and shredded cheese (or any combination of your favourite pizza topping).
5. Return to oven and continue cooking until cheese melts and bubbles.

Sausage with Cabbage

Serves 4

Ingredients:

Butter
1 cup beef broth (one bouillon cube and a cup of water)
1 head cabbage
1 package beef smoked sausage (keilbasa)
3 cloves garlic (I love garlic)
1 medium onion

How you make it:

1. Core the cabbage and chop into approximately 1.5 to 2 inch pieces.

2. Chop onion and sauté in large soup pot, adding minced garlic near the end.

3. Cut sausage into 1/4" thick slices and cook in onion/garlic/butter for about 5 minutes.

4. Spread sausage over bottom of pot evenly and place cabbage on top, and pour in broth

5. Cover, reduce heat, and let steam till cabbage is tender (about 10 to 15 minutes).

6. Stir and serve (salt/pepper to taste of course)

Baked Zucchini Beef

Serves 4

Ingredients:

4 zucchini, cut into 1/4 inch slices
1 cup chopped celery
1 cup chopped onion
1 lb. ground beef
Coconut oil
I cup sliced mushrooms
1 6oz tomato paste
2 cups shredded mozzarella cheese
1 tbsp. salt
1/2 tbsp. oregano
1/4 tbsp. pepper

How you make it:

1. Heat oven to 350.
2. Arrange zucchini in 13x9 baking dish.
3. In fry pan, cook onion and celery in oil for 5 minutes.
4. Add ground beef, cook until it loses its pink color.

Onion Supreme Burger

Serves 8

Ingredients:
1 pkg. Lipton onion soup mix
2 lbs. Hamburger
16 oz. Monterey Jack Cheese w/jalapeno peppers, grated
2 tbsp. Butter
2 tbsp. Masala Cooking Wine
2 lg. Sweet onions, sliced

How you make it:

1. Mix hamburger and soup mix. Form into 8 burgers.
2. Grill until you feel it's done for you or bake on a broiler pan in 350-degree oven for 15 minutes on each side.
3. Slice onions. Melt butter in a frying pan.
4. Add onions and sauté until browned.
5. Add cooking wine and simmer until warm.
6. Pile onions upon cooked hamburgers and top with cheese.
7. Cook in microwave just long enough to melt cheese.

Simple Moussaka

Serves 4

Ingredients:

1.5 lb. ground beef
1 lb. medium eggplant
1 large onion
1 large tomato
4 eggs
2 tsp. coconut Oil
Salt to taste
Sweet paprika
1 tbsp. Black pepper

How you make it:

1. Chop onion, fry in oil until golden, add ground beef, brown, add spices.

2. Cover and simmer, stirring occasionally to keep the bottom from burning, for 1/2 hour.

3. Meanwhile, slice eggplant in 1/4" slices. Fry them on both sides in plenty of oil, until golden. You can try to blot or squeeze out the oil, but eggplant is like sponge, it will sop up a lot of oil. That's a good thing on LC!

4. Line the bottom of a heat-resistant pan with half the fried eggplant slices. Drain the meat, and spread over the eggplant. Cover with the rest of the eggplant slices.

5. Slice the tomato, and layer the slices on top of the eggplant.

6. Cover the pan and bake at 400F for 45 minutes.

7. Take the pan out. Uncover. Crack the eggs on top of the tomato. Try to keep the yolks from breaking.

8.   Return to oven, bake until eggs are as done as you like them.

Pepperoni Beef

Serves 2- 4

Ingredients:

2 tbsp. butter
1 large sweet onion, sliced
1 lb. of kielbasa sausage, sliced in 1/2" pieces
2 med. green peppers, sliced

How you make it:

1. Melt butter in skillet.
2. Add onions and green peppers and sauté until tender.
3. Add the kielbasa and cook until desired doneness. Serve warm.

Delicious Parmesan Beef

Yield: 6 servings

Ingredients:

1 tbsp. Coconut oil
3 cloves garlic; crushed
1 1/2 lb. ground beef round
1/2 tsp. salt
1 cup Parmesan cheese; grated
1/4 tsp. coarsely ground pepper
1/3 cup chopped fresh parsley
1 tbsp. butter
Lemon wedges
1/3 cup chopped parsley

How you make it:

1.   Mix meat-mixture ingredients (first 6) until well blended. Shape into twelve 1 1/4-inch thick patties. Let stand 15 minutes.

2.   Heat oil and butter in a large heavy non-stick skillet over medium-high heat.

3.   Add patties and cook until well browned on both sides and no longer pink in center, about 5 minutes.

4.   Sprinkle with remaining parsley. Serve with lemon wedges to squeeze over the patties.

Southwestern Salad

4 Servings, about 1/2 cup beef mixture, 1/2 cup lettuce and cheese mixture each

Ingredients:

1/2 cup Onions, chopped
1 pound Lean ground beef
1 tablespoon Chili powder
2 teaspoons Dry oregano
1/2 teaspoon Ground cumin
1 cup canned kidney beans, red, drained
1 15-ounce can Canned Garbanzo bean, drained
Tomato, diced 1 medium
Lettuce 2 cups
1/2 cup Cheddar cheese

How you make it:

1. Cook ground beef and onions in a large skillet until the beef no longer remains pink. Drain.
2. Stir oregano, chili powder, and cumin into beef mixture; cook for 1 minute.
3. Add beans, chickpeas, and tomatoes. Mix gently to combine.
4. Combine lettuce and cheese in large serving bowl.
5. Portion lettuce and cheese onto 4 plates.
6. Add 1 cup of beef mixture on top of lettuce and cheese.

Beef n Noodle Casserole

4 Servings, about 2 cups each

Ingredients:
1/2 cup Onions, chopped finely
3 quarts boiling water
1 pound Lean ground beef
Noodles, yolk-free, enriched, uncooked 2-3/4 cups
1 10-3/4-ounce can Tomato soup, condensed
1-1/4 cups Water
1/8 teaspoon Pepper
1 cup Bread crumbs

How you make it:

1. Brown beef and onions in hot skillet; drain.
2. Place water in large saucepan; bring to rolling boil. Cook noodles in boiling water for 10 minutes; drain and set aside.
3. Combine soup, water, and pepper. Stir into cooked meat.
4. Add cooked noodles to meat mixture. Stir gently to avoid tearing the noodles.
5. Spoon beef-noodle mixture into 9- by 13-inch baking pan. Sprinkle bread crumbs over beef-noodle mixture.
6. Bake, uncovered, at 300° F, about 30 minutes.

Chilin Chili

Serves 8

Ingredients:

2 tsp. dried oregano
2 tbsp. olive oil
3 garlic cloves, smashed
1 large onion, chopped
4 lbs. boneless chuck, in dice or ground for chili
1/2 cup ground mild red chile
2 tbsp. ground cumin
1 tsp. cider vinegar
1/2 cup strong brewed coffee or 1 tbsp. instant coffee powder
1 tbsp. sweet paprika
2 tbsp. cornmeal (you can play around with different kinds of thickeners)
3 cups water as needed
1 tbsp. salt
1/2 tsp. ground red pepper (cayenne), optional

How you make it:

1. Heat the oil and cook the onion over medium heat until its soft, in large Dutch oven.
2. Add the garlic and cook until it's transparent.
3. Add the meat in several batches along with the cumin, chile, oregano, and paprika.
4. Remove each batch to a large bowl as it's cooked.
5. Stir and cook until the meat is browned, then put all the meat back in the pot and add the vinegar, coffee, and enough water just to cover the meat.
6. Add the salt and cayenne and stir well.
7. Cover the pot and cook over low heat for 2 hours, stirring from time to time.
8. Remove the lid and simmer for a final hour.
9. Skim off any fat on the surface.
10. Add the cornmeal and stir in well.
11. Cook for 15 more minutes and serve hot in deep bowls.

12. If you desire, garnish with chopped cilantro, sour cream, and/or grated cheese.

Beaf Meatball

4 Servings, about 3 meatballs each, plus 4 servings for another meal

Ingredients:

1/4 cup Onions, minced
1 tablespoon Vegetable oil
2 pounds Lean ground beef
2 Eggs
3/4 cup Bread crumb
1/2 cup Whole milk
1/8 teaspoon Salt
1/2 teaspoon Pepper
2 teaspoons Onion powder
1/2 teaspoon Garlic powder

How you make it:

1. Preheat oven 400° F.
2. Grease baking sheet lightly with oil. Add 1 tablespoon oil and onions to small skillet.
3. Cook over medium heat, until tender, about 3 minutes.
4. Mix remaining ingredients together in bowl; add onions. Mix until blended, using a large serving spoon.
5. Shape beef mixture into 1- to 2-inch meatballs; place on baking sheet.
6. Bake until thoroughly cooked, about 10 to 12 minutes.

Note: Serve with spaghetti sauce and in the meatball sandwich.

World's Greatest Sirloin Stir-Fry

Serves 4

Ingredients:
1 clove garlic, grated
1 pound ground sirloin
1 cup thinly sliced celery, including leaves if available
2 cups sliced mushrooms
2 cups sliced cabbage
1/2 teaspoon dried oregano
2 cups washed and torn spinach
1/4 cup chopped scallions
1 cup mozzarella cheese
1/4 teaspoon ground black pepper

How you make it:

1.   Brown sirloin, mushrooms, garlic, and celery until meat is no longer pink.
2.   Stir in spinach, cabbage, herbs, scallions, and pepper until cabbage and spinach begin to wilt.
3.   Stir in mozzarella and serve.

Arab Meatballs

Serves 8

Ingredients:

1/2 cup finely chopped scallions
2 pounds extra lean ground beef
¾ teaspoon ground cumin
1/4 teaspoon ground cinnamon
1/2 teaspoon ground coriander
1/4 teaspoon ground cayenne pepper
1/2 teaspoon ground black pepper

How you make it:

1. Combine scallions, beef, cumin, cinnamon, coriander, ground black pepper, and ground cayenne pepper.
2. Shape into 24 meatballs.
3. Arrange in baking dish. Bake at 350° until done all the way through , for about 20 minutes.
4. Serve with sour cream if desired.

Baked Meatball

4 Servings, about 3 ounces beef each, plus 4 servings for another meal

Ingredients:

1/2 cup Onion, chopped
2 tablespoons Water
2-1/2 pounds Beef chuck roast, boneless
2 cups Hot water
1 cube Beef bouillon
2 tablespoons Orange juice
1/4 teaspoon Ground allspice
1/8 teaspoon Pepper

How you make it:

1. Preheat oven 400° F.
2. Grease baking sheet lightly with oil. Add 1 tablespoon oil and onions to small skillet.
3. Cook over medium heat, until tender, about 3 minutes.
4. Mix remaining ingredients together in bowl; add onions. Mix until blended, using a large serving spoon.
5. Shape beef mixture into 1- to 2-inch meatballs; place on baking sheet.
6. Bake until thoroughly cooked, about 10 to 12 minutes

Note: Serve with spaghetti sauce and in the meatball sandwich.

Yummy Broiled Chicken

Serves 4

Ingredients:

1 teaspoon salt
1 3-pound frying chicken, quartered
2 tablespoons butter
1 tablespoon lemon juice
1/2 teaspoon crushed dried rosemary leaves
1/4 teaspoon ground black pepper

How you make it:

1. Rub chicken with salt, rosemary, and pepper.
2. Arrange chicken, skin-side down, on broiling pan.
3. Sprinkle with lemon juice. Dot with butter.
4. Broil chicken 25 minutes, about 8 inches from heat source.
5. Baste every 5 minutes with pan drippings.
6. Turn chicken and broil an additional 15 to 20 minutes, until done, basting every 5 minutes with pan drippings.

Baffled Beef Roast

4 Servings, about 3 ounces beef each, plus 4 servings for another meal

Ingredients:

1/2 cup Onion, chopped
2 tablespoons Water
2-1/2 pounds Beef chuck roast, boneless
2 cups Hot water
1 cube Beef bouillon
2 tablespoons Orange juice
1/4 teaspoon Ground allspice
1/8 teaspoon Pepper

How you make it:

1. Simmer onion until tender in 2 tablespoons water in heavy, deep skillet.
2. Add roast to skillet; brown on sides.
3. Combine beef bouillon cube with 2 cups hot water; stir until dissolved.
4. Combine allspice, orange juice, beef broth and pepper. Pour over meat. Cover and simmer, about 2 hours.

Chicken Schnitzel

Servings: 6

Ingredients:

4 slices bacon
1 1/2 pounds boneless, skinless chicken breasts
1 tablespoon finely chopped onion
1 cup sour cream
1 teaspoon paprika

How you make it:

1. Pound the chicken breasts until thin.
2. Cut each breast half in two pieces.
3. Fry bacon until crisp. Add the chicken breasts, and brown in bacon fat.
4. Add onions. Drain fat.
5. Cover pan and continue cooking for 20 minutes.
6. Stir sour cream and paprika, in a small bowl.
7. Pour sour cream over chicken breasts and heat through.

Uptown Burgers

Serves 8

Ingredients:

3 pounds ground beef
1/2 teaspoon ground black pepper
8 slices American cheese
16 slices tomato
8 large lettuce leaves, rinsed and chilled
16 lengthwise slices dill pickle
8 teaspoons mayonnaise

How you make it:

1. Mix ground beef with ground black pepper.
2. Form into 8 patties.
3. Grill until when you feel its done.
4. Arrange individual lettuce leaves on serving plates.
5. Lay 2 slices tomato, 2 slices dill pickle, and a teaspoon of mayonnaise on each lettuce leaf.
6. Place 1 burger on each lettuce leaf, and about a teaspoon of mayonnaise.
7. Wrap lettuce around burger and serve immediately.

10 Checklists For Weight Loss

If you are not getting result in your weight loss pursuit, this are the list of things you need to consider;

1. **CHECK FOR HIDDEN SOURCES OF SUGAR** - Sugar goes under many different names & in many cases does NOT appear on the label. Many vitamin tablets have sugar fillers. CHECK to see the hidden source of sugar you buy in stores!

2. **DON'T GIVE UP** - Your continued search will probably find the problem and correct it. So don't give up, put push harder, because you are only a few step to achieving your weight loss dream.

3. **YOU MAY STILL BE KEEPING YOUR FOOD INTAKE TOO LOW** – Eat at the right time when you are supposed to eat. Many times you carry over habits from other diets & eat too little. EAT UP... The right things & don't skip meals.

4. **PERHAPS YOU'RE CHEATING ON THE DIET** - If you think it's too small to matter, better check again. Instead of 'cheat days' give yourself one 'cheat meal' a week.

5.   **YOU MAY NOT HAVE FOUND YOUR PROPER LEVEL YET** – Reduce the rate of carbs intake still further, works in 4 out of 5 people, or ADD carbs while still remaining in ketosis. Try it and see.

6.   **ARE YOU EATING SIX SMALL MEALS OR SNACKS A DAY?** – A frequent eating schedule will provide a constant source of energy without the insulin rebound. Six small feedings a day are better than 3 large meals to break the energy/weight loss barrier.

7.   **CHECK YOUR MINERAL BALANCE** - You may have a mineral imbalance. Such as zinc/copper. Or a trace mineral shortage.

8.   **TRY TO EXERCISE MORE** - Exercise can improve circulation; stabilize blood sugar & other important metabolic benefits.

9.   **YOU MAY BE LOSING TOO MUCH SALT** - Salt or potassium shortages are common in the first stages of the diet. Eat salty foods & take potassium supplements.

10.   **SEX HORMONES** - Will slow down weight loss and stimulate the production of insulin. Estrogen (used in birth control pills) and Testosterone have much the same effect.

Food Weights, Measurement and Equivalencies

One Equal tablet = one teaspoon of sugar in sweetness, same as one teaspoon of bulk Splenda. However, 30 teaspoons of Splenda will have 12 more grams than 30 Equal tablets.

6 packets == one quarter cup sugar or Splenda

12 packets == one half cup "

24 packets == one cup

Stevia is another matter entirely, and if you have a very well refined stevioside extract, 1/4 tsp. could be equivalent to a cup of sugar, but Stevia's strength varies widely by product.

2 tablespoons butter = 1 ounce

1 stick of butter = 1/4 pound = 1/2 cup

1 square of chocolate -= 1 ounce

Juice of one lemon = 3 to 4 tablespoons

Grated peel of one lemon = 1 teaspoon

One pound cheese, shredded = 4 cups

1/4 pound blue cheese, crumbled = 3/4 to 1 cup

3 teaspoons = 1 tablespoon

4 tablespoons = 1/4 cup

5 1/3 tablespoons = 1/3 cup

16 tablespoons = 1 cup

1 cup = 8 fluid ounces = 1/2 pint

4 cups = 2 pints = 1 quart

4 quarts = 1 gallon

8 quarts = 1 peck

4 pecks = 1 bushel

Kitchen Tips and Tricks You Should Know

To prepare your meat in style, drizzle sauces on the plate in random patterns and place the meat on top

Some recipes include a step where you place semi-solid cheesecake or mousse in a bowl for individual servings; try moulding the dessert with your spoon. Swirly onion-dome peaks can be pretty.

Cut a slice of cheese into a fancy shape e.g. star, flower etc. and place it on top of a cooked chicken breast or hamburger. Run it under the broiler for several seconds-- just long enough so the cheese gets hot and a little puffy, but not so long that it starts to run (which would spoil the shape).

Making no-bake cheesecakes in a mould, is the best way to get them done, if you like no-bake cheesecakes

To make quick breakfast rollups - 1 slice bacon, 1 slice roast turkey, and 1 slice pepper cheese (add lettuce if you like). A nice change, you would like this!

Seafood omelettes using either frozen crabmeat or those little bitty shrimp. Frozen is easiest & cheapest to deal with but if you have fresh available, even better. A little Swiss or Parmesan cheese and you'll never look at bacon the same way again.

Take a small package of cream cheese, cut into chunks. Fry up some bulk sausage, set it aside. Sauté some chopped up onions in the sausage grease, drain and put the sausage back in the pan. Prepare eggs to scramble and pour them over the sausage, cook over medium heat and add the chunks of cream cheese and let it melt into the scramble mixture. The amount you include in this quick breakfast is according to your desired taste.

Here's a quick and easy breakfast: Cottage cheese mix in a packet of equal and a tad bit of cinnamon.

Here's some breakfast ideas: peanut butter, cheese, cream cheese, meat; cottage cheese; make-ahead crust less quiche -- eat cold or zap in microwave for a minute; egg salad, tuna salad, chicken salad

Celery stalks with cream cheese and smoked salmon.YUM! Or sometimes just a bit of sugar-free peanut butter instead of the fancy stuff. Leftover meat, warmed up in the microwave

When making devilled eggs put the filling in a baggie and use shears to cut the edge so you have pretty egg filling and don't have to use a pastry bag.

Hollow out cherry tomatoes and fill with tuna salad, salmon cream cheese, chicken salad, and have a bunch of bite size snacks for the day

The one and only kitchen tip I can give is to always keep a fire extinguisher handy

Conclusion

Fats are the foundation for cell membranes –including the cells in our brains. In fact, fat is critical to brain development and maintenance, and provides the building blocks for cell membranes needed for important work to be performed by neurotransmitters which are responsible for regulation of our moods.

Fats are needed for the manufacturing of hormones and prostaglandins that regulate bodily functions like immune system function, digestion, and reproductive activity. Fats keep the digestive tract working smoothly and balance blood sugar levels.

Fats are necessary to keep our body temperature regulated, protecting internal organs from damage, and allow us to have continuous levels of energy through the day Fats are not only essential to life, but they provide fantastic flavor, too!

All fats are not bad. So dairy products are good because they supply good fats to the body. Moreover, because of being rich in vitamins and minerals, dairy products are good for weight loss as well as for overall health of the body. However, you should remember that you can only maintain healthy weight if you eat real foods and steer clear of junk or processed foods.

If you enjoyed this book, please take the time to share your thoughts and post a positive review with 5 star rating on Amazon, it would encourage me and make me serve you better. It'd be greatly appreciated!

Thank You

Other Health Related Book You Should Get

Other HEalth ReLaTed Books YoU'll LiKe

RECOMMENDED BOOK FROM THE SAME AUTHOR:

As Seen on T.V- <u>Super Shred Diet Recipes: 61 Easy-to-cook Healthy Recipes To Help you Lose weight FAST in 4weeks.</u> This Book would give you lovely Recipe Ideas for Dr. Ian Smith Super Shred Program.

CLICK HERE TO BUY:

http://www.amazon.com/dp/B00HSLG0G8

Are you looking for a Way to lose weight and keep it off for a long time while deepening your relationship with God? Then this is for you,

Get Daniel Fast Shred Diet Recipes: 35 Easy-To-Cook healthy recipes, lose 7 pounds in 7 days on the Daniel Plan. For Just $0.99 Today, for a limited Time.

Lose 7 pounds in 7 days, discover the insider secret... Click on the Link below to buy Now.

http://www.amazon.com/Daniel-Shred-Recipes-Easy---Cook-ebook/dp/B00IADVBIO/

Who else wants to Experience the Incredible taste of the World's Best Sauce...?

Welcome the Brand New, Never Heard Before -The Ultimate Sriracha Hot Sauce- 25 Easy-to-Cook Healthy Recipes with This "Rooster Sauce"

CLICK HERE TO BUY:

http://www.amazon.com/dp/B00HLJWWIQ

The Pound a Day Diet Recipes: 61 easy-to-cook healthy Recipes to Help with Your Diet On A Budget...Loose that pound today eating the foods you love

Recommended for the Pound a Day Dieters

CLICK HERE TO BUY ON AMAZON:

http://bookShow.me/B00HXYU736

Books on Health & Fitness Diets

RECOMMENDED BOOK FOR WEIGHT LOSS AND DIET:

My 10-Day Smoothie Cleanse & Detox Diet Cookbook: Burn the Fat, Lose weight Fast and Boost your Metabolism for Busy Mom, Restart your life with this cookbook and experience an amazing transformation of your body and your health. I am really excited for you!

CLICK HERE TO BUY: http://www.amazon.com/10-Day-Detox-Diet-Cookbook-Metabolism-ebook/dp/B00IRE3CV0

Get this bestselling Grain Brain Book- **My brain against all grain Cookbook: 61 Easy-to-make Healthy Foods that would help you stick to the Grain-Brain-free Diet!** Discover The Surprising Truth about Wheat, Carbs, and Sugar--Your Brain's Silent Killers

Amazon US Link: http://www.amazon.com/dp/B00J9DX3X0

Amazon UK Link: http://www.amazon.co.uk/dp/B00J9DX3X0

The Coconut Diet Cookbook: Using Coconut Oil to Lose weight FAST, Supercharge Your Metabolism & Look Beautiful!

Link http://www.amazon.com/dp/BooK1IIOGS

Made in the USA
Lexington, KY
02 July 2014